CH

values

Patriotism

www.av2books.com

**Cynthia Amoroso
and Emma Thompson**

LET'S READ
AV²
BY WEIGL™
ADDED VALUE • AUDIO VISUAL

Go to **www.av2books.com**, and enter this book's unique code.

BOOK CODE

X 6 8 4 8 4 7

AV² **by Weigl** brings you media enhanced books that support active learning.

AV² provides enriched content that supplements and complements this book. Weigl's AV² books strive to create inspired learning and engage young minds in a total learning experience.

Your AV² Media Enhanced books come alive with...

Audio
Listen to sections of the book read aloud.

Video
Watch informative video clips.

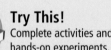
Embedded Weblinks
Gain additional information for research.

Try This!
Complete activities and hands-on experiments.

Key Words
Study vocabulary, and complete a matching word activity.

Quizzes
Test your knowledge.

Slide Show
View images and captions, and prepare a presentation.

... and much, much more!

Published by AV² by Weigl
350 5th Avenue, 59th Floor New York, NY 10118
Website: www.av2books.com

Project Coordinator: Emma Thompson
Art Director: Terry Paulhus

Every reasonable effort has been made to trace ownership and to obtain permission to reprint copyright material. The publisher would be pleased to have any errors or omissions brought to its attention so that they may be corrected in subsequent printings.

The publisher acknowledges Getty Images, Alamy, and Shutterstock as the primary image suppliers for this title.

Library of Congress Control Number: 2017930870

ISBN 978-1-4896-6073-2 (hardcover)
ISBN 978-1-4896-6074-9 (softcover)
ISBN 978-1-4896-6075-6 (multi-user eBook)

Printed in the United States of America in Brainerd, Minnesota
1 2 3 4 5 6 7 8 9 0 21 20 19 18 17

032017
020317

CONTENTS

What Is Patriotism?   5

Patriotism in Words   6

Patriotism and Flags   9

Patriotism and Music   10

Patriotism and Parades   13

Patriotism and Voting   14

Keeping Countries Safe   17

Patriotism and You   18

Patriotism Makes You Stronger   21

Key Words   22

Index   23

What You've Learned/
AV2books.com   24

What Is Patriotism?

Patriotism is a feeling of love and respect for your country. There are lots of different countries in the world. Most people love the land in which they live. They are proud of it. They show their patriotism in many different ways.

People show patriotism by dressing in their country's colors.

Patriotism in Words

People often put their feelings of patriotism into words. They might write poems about their country. They might talk about the beauty of their land. Or they might write about its past. They might talk about making it a better place. They might make a pledge to keep it safe.

American schoolchildren often say the Pledge of Allegiance.

Patriotism and Flags

Each country has its own flag. The flag is a **symbol** for the country. Flags come in all colors and patterns. The colors and patterns stand for different things. People are proud of their country's flag. They fly their flag to show their patriotism.

Schools across the United States fly the American flag.

Patriotism and Music

People often write or play music to honor their country. Often the music has words. Sometimes it does not. Each country has its own **anthem**. An anthem is a special song that honors the country. The anthem of the United States is "The Star-Spangled Banner."

The national anthem is performed before some sporting events.

Patriotism and Parades

People often show patriotism in parades. They carry their nation's flags. Sometimes they wear their nation's colors. Many countries hold parades on special days. Often these are days when important things happened in the country's past.

Americans often hold parades on the Fourth of July.

Patriotism and Voting

Many countries hold **elections** to choose their leaders. People vote for the person they think will do the best job. The person who gets the most votes wins. Voting gives everyone a say in how things should be done. It is a special way of showing patriotism.

Signs tell people where they can vote.

Keeping Countries Safe

Some people have special jobs keeping their countries safe. Many of them serve in the **military.** They try to keep the nation from being attacked. If they need to, they fight for their land. Many people show their patriotism by doing this job.

American soldiers promise to protect their country.

Patriotism and You

How can you show patriotism? Learning about your country is a great place to start! You can learn about your nation's past. You can learn about its land and people. You can learn how its **government** works. You can learn what problems it faces today. You can think about how to make it better.

Schoolchildren all over the world learn about their own countries.

Patriotism Makes You Stronger

People everywhere want good places to live. They have different ideas about what their countries should be like. But they show patriotism by doing their part. They work to make their countries better and stronger.

Your country is a big part of who you are.

Key Words

anthem: An anthem is a national song.

elections: In elections, people vote to pick their leaders.

government: A group of people in charge of running a country.

military: An army of people who are ready to protect their country.

symbol: Something that stands for something else.

Index

anthem 10

colors 5, 9, 13

elections 14

flags 9, 13

government 18

job 14, 17

military 17
music 10

parades 13
Pledge of Allegiance 6
poems 6
proud 5, 9

symbol 8

vote 14

What You've Learned

People show patriotism by dressing in their country's colors.

American schoolchildren often say the Pledge of Allegiance.

Schools across the United States fly the American flag.

The national anthem is performed before some sporting events.

Americans often hold parades on the Fourth of July.

Signs tell people where they can vote.

American soldiers promise to protect their country.

Schoolchildren all over the world learn about their own countries.

Your country is a big part of who you are.

Check out www.av2books.com for activities, videos, audio clips, and more!

1 Go to www.av2books.com.

2 Enter book code. **X 6 8 4 8 4 7**

3 Fuel your imagination online!

www.av2books.com